Praise. Laugh. Repeat.

DEVOTIONAL

TED SHUTTLESWORTH JR.

Published in Virginia Beach, Virginia by Miracle Word Publishing.

Miracle Word titles may be purchased in bulk for educational, business, fund-
raising, or sales promotional use. For information, please e-mail info@mira-
cleword.com

Unless otherwise indicated, all Scripture quotations are taken from the Holy
Bible, New Living Translation, copyright © 1996, 2004, 2007, 2013 by Tyndale
House Foundation. Used by permission of Tyndale House Publishers, Inc., Carol
Stream, Illinois 60188. All rights reserved.

Scripture quotations marked KJV are from THE KING JAMES VERSION of the
Bible, public domain.

Scripture quotations marked NKJV are from the NEW KING JAMES VERSION.
© 1982 by Thomas Nelson, Inc. Used by permission. All rights reserved.

Scripture quotations taken from the New American Standard Bible®, Copyright
© 1960, 1962, 1963, 1968, 1971, 1972, 1973, 1975, 1977, 1995 by The Lockman
Foundation Used by permission." (www.Lockman.org)

Scripture quotations marked (AMP) are taken from the Amplified Bible,
Copyright © 1954, 1958, 1962, 1964, 1965, 1987 by The Lockman Foundation.
Used by permission.

All uppercase and italicized text in verses of scripture are added by the author
for the purpose of emphasis.

ISBN 978-0-9909196-1-2

Printed in the United States of America

CONTENTS

JOY COMES IN THE MORNING

One of the things that has bothered me the most in the time that I've been ministering for the Lord is seeing people's lives destroyed by depression and anxiety.

I was tired of preaching at youth events and seeing young girls at the altar with their sleeves rolled up showing me the cut marks on their arms.

From the wrists to the elbows they were scarred with cuts from knives, needles and glass. The devil had lied to them and made them feel worthless.

I was sick of seeing young men and women who were in a constant fight for their life. Anxiety and depression had pushed them to contemplate suicide on a daily basis.

When God first started giving me the *Praise. Laugh.*

Repeat. message, I felt it was a holy response to the evil things the enemy was doing to our generation.

The Bible says, "weeping may endure for a night." God has not designed His children to go through life enduring struggle after struggle.

You are not ordained to spend years trying to break free from the evil that the enemy has sent to destroy you. In fact, when Jesus found a woman who had been bound for eighteen years, He broke tradition and healed her on the sabbath day. (Luke 13:13).

He believed it was not right to allow her to suffer any longer once He had been made aware of her issue.

That principle remains. It is not right for God's children to suffer month after month and year after year.

Joy comes in the morning.

This 40-day devotional companion to *Praise. Laugh. Repeat.* is designed to guide you through the Word of God on a course that will keep you in overwhelming joy.

What you're about to read is not a rehashing of what I wrote in the preceding book. This devotional is filled with additional material that God gave me during times of prayer and fasting.

I encourage you to read this with your Bible, a pen and notebook, or a tablet. God will open your eyes to the wonders of His goodness as you study His Word.

I pray that when these forty days are finished you will have experienced a supernatural transformation.

May God fuel your purpose with Heaven's happiness. There truly is nothing like the overwhelming joy of the Lord.

It's unspeakable.

It's full of glory.

Ted Shuttlesworth Jr.
April 2015

DAY ONE
BURN THE ROLLER COASTER

....

"For the kingdom of God is not eating and drinking, but righteousness and peace and joy in the Holy Spirit."
—ROMANS 14:17 NASB

Today's Bible reading: Romans 14:12–18

Have you ever considered the thought that you are a major contributor to someone else's joy? I believe that God has set us in this world and given us the relationships we have for a reason. I like to call it our *"circle of influence."*

Just as we understand that our heavenly Father expects us to be good stewards of other areas of our lives like finances and time, we should also realize that He expects us to steward relationships properly.

That means utilizing the fruit of the Spirit when we interact with those around us. The passage we read today in the book of Romans encourages us to "live in such a way that you will not cause another believer to stumble and fall." (Romans 14:13).

There are so many people surrounding you that are in need of the true joy of the Holy Spirit. Make it your mission to become a fountain of joy that will encourage them at all times.

That means you can't afford to fall into the trap of becoming the emotional roller coaster that many people end up riding. Emotional roller coasters, like real ones, always end up back where they started. There's no real progress.

Let's be honest, sometimes it's easier to just let yourself go when you're going through something that takes faith to overcome. These are the very moments that define your influence in the lives of those with whom God has entrusted you.

Emotional roller coasters, like real ones, always end up back where they started. There's no real progress.
#PraiseLaughRepeat

The strength of your personal joy solidifies your position to help those in need around you. One of the most wonderful things about being filled with the wonderful joy of the Holy Spirit is that it makes you a lighthouse standing firm on the shore. While the enemy would love to distract those around you with the storms of life until they crash onto the jagged rocks of eternity, the power of God in you directs them to safety.

It's time to begin activating your joy and bringing encouragement and strength to your *circle of influence.*

The Holy Spirit will empower you to lift the burdens of life from the shoulders of the ones you love. Begin today and burn the emotional roller coaster.

....

PRAYER POINT: Heavenly Father, empower me with the joy of the Holy Spirit so that I can immediately begin to bring change to those around me. I commit myself to a lifestyle of joy.

....

DAY TWO

THE PLAYBOOK

....

"You will make known to me the path of life; In Your presence is fullness of joy; In Your right hand there are pleasures forever."

—PSALM 16:11 NASB

Today's Bible reading: Psalm 16:7–11

King David knew something about God that made him a very successful man. He knew that the Lord was his Shepherd. His Guide. In fact, when he said, "early will I seek you; my soul thirsts for you," he was making a dedicated effort to ensure God was the first person he talked to every single day. (Psalm 63:1 NKJV).

In this extremely busy society we live in, it's easy to miss out on the most important event of the day: talking to God. If we never speak to Him, we'll miss out on hearing what He has to say regarding our personal path of life.

Everyone's life is different. So although the Bible is

a wonderful resource to guide us in a general way, it's not a standalone solution for the life of the believer. This is why God sent us the Holy Spirit as a personal guide for our lives. By speaking to Him we have the ability to uncover the secrets that He has set aside for us.

The fact that you're reading this devotional and have dedicated yourself to seeking the plan of God for your life is a sign that you're on the right track!

Notice in today's verse that there is eternal pleasure in discovering the path of your life from God. It's not His desire that we stumble randomly through life. He has already laid out perfect steps for us to walk. (Psalm 37:23).

Until talking to God becomes more important than binge-watching Netflix, we'll coast through life missing our blessings. #PraiseLaughRepeat

You have to decide that talking to God is more important than Netflix, Facebook, XBox, Playstation, your iPhone, tablet, the mall, the movies, your friends and anything else that doesn't have the power to change your destiny. Until talking to God becomes more important than binge-watching Netflix, we'll coast through life missing our blessings.

God has wonderful things set aside for us, but until we discover what they are, we can't obtain them. Receiving the everlasting pleasures of God brings an infusion of joy.

So do whatever it takes to dedicate yourself to talking to God. Tie a string to your finger, put a sticky note on your mirror, program an alarm in your phone, or tattoo it on your forehead. (Don't do the last one.)

I once heard someone say that if you make an appointment to meet with God, He'll never miss it and He'll never be late. Schedule your appointment.

....

PRAYER POINT: Heavenly Father, give me a supernatural hunger to pray and read Your Word. I ask You to reveal to me Your customized path for my life.

....

3

DAY THREE

EAT THIS, NOT THAT

*"Your words were found and I ate
them, And Your words became for me
a joy and the delight of my heart;"*
—JEREMIAH 15:16 NASB

Today's Bible reading: Proverbs 4:18-23

So much is said in our generation about what we should
eat. We are bombarded with suggestions everywhere we
go. The sights and smells mixed with society's sugges-
tion that we should always be eating something makes
for a daily struggle.

If that weren't enough, we can't even enjoy what we
eat because every magazine, TV show, and article on the
internet is telling us why what we just ate is probably
going to end up killing us.

Author David Zinczenko, who wrote *Eat This, Not
That!*, did his best to simplify our choices and help us to
make a conscious effort to eat healthier.

7

In the same way, God gave us instructions through-out His Word regarding what we should eat spiritually. You'll find in our reading from Proverbs today that God considers His Word to be spiritual nutrition.

When you ingest it on a regular basis you will find, as the prophet Jeremiah did, that His Word will not only be health, but also joy to your heart.

God's Word is literally His medicine for your body. It's the only prescrip-tion you need. #PraiseLaughRepeat

Not only does your spirit benefit from reading Scrip-ture, your body will also gain strength. God's Word is literally His medicine for your body. It's the only pre-scription you need.

I want to encourage you to not let your daily study of the Bible stop with this devotional experience. Dedi-cate yourself to dig deeper into the treasure found with-in God's Word.

It's important to realize that everything that we re-ceive from God is based upon what we receive from His Word.

Many people don't read the Bible more often be-cause they feel like they can't understand it. Sometimes they are reading a translation of the Bible that's hard to understand like the King James Version. I always encourage Christians to find a version of Scripture that they can understand and enjoy reading. I usually recommend the New Living Translation, English Standard Version or the New American Standard Version.

It does you no good to read the Bible if you don't understand what you're reading. In fact, Jesus said that having no understanding is one of the reasons that the devil can steal the blessings of God from your life. (Matthew 13:19). It's very important to understand what you read.

Your life will explode with the wonderful blessings of Heaven as you study God's Word and fill your heart with the promises of God.

Let a hunger and desire to be filled with God's Word be birthed in your heart today!

....

PRAYER POINT: Heavenly Father, give me a supernatural hunger to read Your Word. I ask You to open my spiritual eyes and give me an uncommon understanding of what I'm reading.

....

4

DAY FOUR

THE WRONG CLOTHES CAN KILL YOU

....

"To console those who mourn in Zion,
To give them . . .The garment of praise
for the spirit of heaviness . . ."
— ISAIAH 61:3 NKJV

Today's Bible reading: Isaiah 61:1-11

When you hear the word "praise" you probably think of your favorite Christian album or possibly the part of the church service before the preaching begins.

Although singing and music are one form of praise, it's not reserved for those times alone. In fact, we are instructed to live a lifestyle of praise toward God.

David said, "I will praise the Lord at all times. I will constantly speak his praises." (Psalm 34:1).

Praise isn't reserved for the right moment when your life is at it's best. It isn't an emotional response to prime conditions. Praise is a choice.

When you choose to praise God, you're making a

conscious decision to involve God in your situation. Praise is a tool given to us by God that engages heavenly assistance on our behalf.

By praising God you illicit a response from Heaven. Prayer is a powerful tool that we should always use in our lives, but it's not enough. Praise is the catalyst that makes your prayers explode.

Maybe you've seen someone who has built a miniature volcano as a science project or possibly built one yourself. After the paper mache or plaster is formed into a mountainous shape that is the frame of the volcano, you have to create the lava that flows out of the top.

To create the illusion of lava flowing out of the volcano, you have to mix two ingredients: baking soda and vinegar. You can leave the baking soda in the volcano forever and it will never erupt, but when the vinegar is added the mixture produces the flowing lava effect.

....

 Praise is a tool given to us by God that engages heavenly assistance on our behalf. #PraiseLaughRepeat

....

Praise is the catalyst that causes your prayers to be explosively answered and overwhelming joy to flood your life.

The enemy's desire is to keep you in a constant state

of heaviness. That heaviness becomes a never-ending anxiety and depression that holds you prisoner.

Thanks to the power of the Holy Spirit, we can choose to strip off what the Bible calls a "spirit of heaviness" and put on the "garment of praise." Wear it proudly like a new pair of shoes. Don't be embarrassed that you love Jesus. Praise God every chance you get.

Start by removing things that allow heaviness to fill your life, e.g. depressing music, wrong relationships or even attending a dead church.

Fill your mind and heart with the uplifting promises of God's Word. Sing praise to God. Pray and talk to Him as often as you can, and for crying out loud, find a church that is on fire. What if you can't find one in the area where you live?

Move.

PRAYER POINT: Heavenly Father, thank You for giving me the weapon of praise. Give me a constant awareness of Your Presence and a desire to praise you at all times and on every possible occasion.

5

DAY FIVE

LAUGHING OUTSIDE CRYING INSIDE

....

*"Even in laughter the heart may ache,
and the end of joy may be grief."*
—PROVERBS 14:13 ESV

Today's Bible reading: Proverbs 14:1–35

Not everyone who is laughing has the joy of the Lord. In fact, you may be surprised to find out how many people who look happy are actually hurting.

Many people put on a facade and pretend like everything in their life is fine while the opposite is true. Things may be falling apart for them.

Never mistake laughter for joy. Laughter is merely one of the effects joy has on you. True joy may also cause singing, dancing, rejoicing, sharing your faith, giving and many other outward signs.

The cause is the fountain of joy springing up on the inside of your heart.

The devil doesn't mind if you laugh as long as there's no true joy deposited in your life from Heaven. He doesn't care if you fake it for awhile as long as he can keep you in bondage before, during and after your laughter.

As you are empowered with Heaven's happiness, God will use you to bring that freedom to someone else. Don't be put off by the fact that they appear to be happy. When God is leading you to help someone, He knows the internal struggles they're battling.

The devil doesn't care if you laugh as long as he can keep you in bondage before, during and after your laughter. #PraiseLaughRepeat

Once, while preaching a youth conference, I felt to minister to a young man at the altar. He looked healthy, strong and absolutely fine to me.

As I began to minister to him, God led me to rebuke a spirit of depression and anxiety. He didn't look depressed or sad at all. As I laid hands on him he began to jump and shout.

After the service he shared with me that he had contemplated and almost committed suicide the week before the conference.

God knew what he needed. Freedom came to him that night and I was able to minister to him by the leading of the Holy Spirit.

I believe God is going to use you to bring help and healing to those whose lives are void of supernatural joy. Always remember that you cannot judge what someone needs or is believing for by their appearance.

The enemy may try to keep them caged up on the inside, but God has anointed you to liberate every captive. Now that you are free, you're in position to help others that remain in chains of bondage. (Luke 4:18).

PRAYER POINT: Heavenly Father, empower me to break the chains of depression and anxiety off of those around me. Use me to bring freedom to my friends and family by the leading of Your Spirit.

THE STRONGEST SPIRIT WINS

....

"For God has not given us a spirit of fear, but of power and of love and of a sound mind."

— 2 TIMOTHY 1:7 NKJV

Today's Bible reading: 2 Timothy 1:7–18

Fear is not a state of mind. Anxiety is not merely a mental disorder. The Bible tells us that fear is a spirit. The issue we face in this generation is that we've tried to diagnose spiritual conditions and cure them with natural medications which doesn't work.

Spirits don't respond to antidepressants. Any spiritual problem must be dealt with spiritually. Paul was telling Timothy that God has given us power, love and a sound mind, which are also spirits, to combat the spirit of fear.

The devil is playing an eternal game of "King of the Hill" with every individual on the planet. Some people lose while other people build up enough spiritual strength to throw the devil off of their hill and stand victorious at the top.

The devil only respects power. This is why he doesn't answer to every Christian in the same way. (Acts 19:15–16). You have to build sufficient spiritual strength to overcome him when the day of battle arrives. (Proverbs 24:10). If you don't, even as a Christian you will lose battles.

> Being a Christian doesn't mean you'll never have to fight again, it means you finally have the proper weapons to win. #PraiseLaughRepeat

As author Jack London wrote in *The Call of the Wild*, you must learn to "survive triumphantly in a hostile environment where only the strong survive."

This means accessing a supernatural spirit of power to win in the day of battle. Being a Christian doesn't mean you'll never have to fight again, it means you finally have the proper weapons to win.

Sometimes people get angry with me in this politically correct society and try to paint me as irresponsible because I look at issues from a spiritual viewpoint. Some have told me that it's foolish to ignore the diagnoses of medical specialists.

As Christians we need to be aware of the reality of the supernatural realm. It's dangerous to mistake spiritual problems as natural ones. When you treat or medicate a spiritual issue you're only dealing with the effect and never the cause.

Prayer and praise are the quickest ways to build supernatural strength to overcome in battle. (Mark 9:29 / Acts 16:25). When you pray you are accessing your heavenly account. You're making withdrawals like you would with a debit card at your bank.

Praise is the other side of the coin that causes God's power to be activated on your behalf. (Psalm 22:3) As we previously discussed, praise causes the power of your prayer to explode.

Begin building your personal power supply today and prepare to rejoice as you win every battle that you fight.

....

PRAYER POINT: Heavenly Father, give me an awareness of the unseen realm around me. Lead me to pray and build my spiritual power level to win every battle by faith.

....

7

DAY SEVEN

HEAVEN'S PHARMACY

*"A happy heart is good medicine and
a cheerful mind works healing, but a
broken spirit dries up the bones."*
—PROVERBS 17:22 AMP

Today's Bible reading: Proverbs 17:1–28

I am always amazed to read this scripture about how
the joy of the Lord is literal medicine to your body. As
time moves forward and more research is conducted,
modern science is confirming what was written by King
Solomon over 1,300 years ago.

Recently, Dr. Lee Berk and Dr. Stanley Tan of Loma
Linda University found that laughter can lower blood
pressure, reduce stress hormones, improve cardiac
health, boost T cells, release natural pain killers called
endorphins, and more.

At an even greater level, the healing power of supernatural joy goes above and beyond the abilities of

laughter because it is a wellspring found in the presence of God. (Psalm 16:11). The very presence of God brings healing to the body.

A 2013 Gallup poll showed that 51% of adults in America take a multivitamin every day because they believe it is beneficial to their overall health.

I find it interesting that Christians will take a vitamin every day, convinced that it will increase their health, but many neglect regular access to the presence of God which ensures divine healing.

Make a decision to fill your prescription on a daily basis by entering into the joy of the Lord. The time you spend in the presence of God is the most valuable investment you will make each day.

In that meeting with the Holy Spirit you will receive fresh instructions, strength to accomplish your purpose, overwhelming joy, healing for your body, divine wisdom and guidance.

....

The time you spend in the presence of God is the most valuable investment you will make each day.
#PraiseLaughRepeat

....

Have you ever wondered why the devil works so hard to keep you out of the presence of God? He uses the frustrations and anxieties of the natural world to rob you of fellowship with the Lord. (Mark 4:18–19).

Now that we're realizing how many illnesses and relationship failures are centered around stress, we understand the scope of our enemy's plan. He wants us walking around with broken spirits and dried up bones.

Today is the day to determine that you will not be a walking bag of dry, dusty bones. You have to purposefully decide to access Heaven's pharmacy and fill your joy prescription daily.

Depending on Heaven's health care system is the best decision you could ever make. God will never fail you.

....

PRAYER POINT: Heavenly Father, fill me with the healing medicine of Heaven as I enter Your presence today. Keep me free from every plan and plot of my enemy, in Jesus name.

....

8

DAY EIGHT

WHERE ARE THE REFRESHMENTS?

*"With joy you will drink deeply from
the fountain of salvation!"*

— ISAIAH 12:3 NLT

Today's Bible reading: Isaiah 12:1–6

Christianity is not hard. Let's get that out of the way at
the very beginning today. Some people act like it's hard,
but Jesus said it's not. (Matthew 11:30).

Have you ever met that Christian? The one who has
a sour look on their face as though the more bitter they
become the more pious they will be. What a sad advertisement to the sinner.

Christianity is only frustrating when you refuse to
use the tools and resources that have been provided by
the Holy Spirit.

My family is full of great cooks. We are kind of over
the top in our preparation and presentation of food.

When the holidays come you can forget it. You'd think an army was coming to eat from the appetizers that are laid out. In reality, however, it's only going to be nine or ten people.

By the time dinner is ready we're completely stuffed with all of the amazing appetizers that covered every square inch of the counters and tables.

Those experiences have pretty much ruined me when eating elsewhere. Even my subconscious expectations are way too high. Once you've had fresh lobster stew, massive shrimp and crab cake sliders, old pepperoni slices laid on top of stale Ritz crackers don't hold the same appeal. I want to be filled, not frustrated.

The same is true in the Kingdom of God. Your life in Christ is designed to be enjoyed and leave you refreshed and satisfied.

Salvation is a fountain to refresh you
not a desert to distress you.
#PraiseLaughRepeat

The Prophet Isaiah wrote that we would drink deeply from the fountain of salvation with joy.

Notice that salvation is a fountain to refresh you and not a desert to distress you.

God has given you His gladness as the cup to enjoy

the full benefits of salvation. Understand that without joy you have nothing to use to draw the benefits from your salvation.

If you are not personally refreshed by the Spirit of God, you do not have the ability to refresh anyone else. One of the most vital components of your purpose is the refreshing peace and joy of the Lord.

When unbelievers see what wonderful things God is doing in your life, it creates an interest in His goodness. (Romans 2:4).

Always remember that you are a walking advertisement for the goodness and mercy of God. Make up your mind to show others how good it is to serve the King of kings. Lead them to the refreshments.

PRAYER POINT: Heavenly Father, refresh me today by Your power and give me the ability to become a fountain of refreshing for others.

DESTINY JUICE

*"Don't be dejected and sad, for the joy
of the Lord is your strength!"*
—NEHEMIAH 8:10 NLT

Today's Bible reading: Nehemiah 8:1-11

Marketing is such a powerful tool that the messages we receive about products stick with us for a long time. When I was growing up, major sports personalities like Michael Jordan received endorsements from companies like Wheaties to sell their cereal.

We were supposed to believe if you at your Wheaties and bought Nike Air Jordan shoes that you could perform like Michael Jordan.

Unfortunately not.

Although it's important to eat a healthy diet, there is no product that's going to launch you into superproductivity. Red Bull does not, in fact, give you wings.

Wouldn't it be easier if you could just chug one drink and your abilities jump up to the next level?

Believe it or not, God did give us a substance to use that would boost our energies and be the fuel that allows us to accomplish our purpose with momentum and force.

Joy is your destiny juice.

The Bible tells us that joy equals strength. In context, the people of God were accomplishing their purpose with a momentum that made their enemies nervous.

A believer who remains in the joy of the Lord is an unstoppable force. If the devil cannot weaken you, he can't defeat you or hold you back from your God-given destiny.

Praise is not just a natural response to God's goodness, it's a spiritual transaction that provokes God to action. #PraiseLaughRepeat

Nothing is more detrimental to your future than to neglect the act of praising God. Praise is not just a natural response to God's goodness, it's a spiritual transaction that provokes God to action.

One of the biggest mistakes the nation of Israel made while in captivity was refusing to engage in praise unto

God. They allowed their circumstances to govern their song instead of letting their song change their circumstances.

They put away their harps by hanging them on willow trees and abandoned the songs of Zion. (Psalm 137:2-4). Don't hang up your harp. To put it in the words of Kool and the Gang, "Get your back up off the wall."

The more time you dedicate to praising God the higher your joy level rises. Your joy needs to be maintained with care to ensure your strength level is sufficient for success in the Kingdom.

....

PRAYER POINT: Heavenly Father, I thank You that my strength comes from Heaven. As I praise You today give me supernatural strength to accomplish what You've called me to do.

....

DAY TEN

WHAT'S IN A NAME?

"You haven't done this before. Ask, using my name, and you will receive, and you will have abundant joy."

—JOHN 16:24 NLT

Today's Bible reading: John 16:16–33

One of the popular quotes that has come from Shakespeare's classic *Romeo and Juliet* was spoken by Juliet in act two when she says, "What's in a name? That which we call a rose by any other name would smell as sweet."

The point Shakespeare is trying to make through his character is that names are really just labels that don't mean anything.

He couldn't be more wrong.

In fact, Jesus gives His disciples a secret key to answered prayer in John chapter 16. He says, "Ask using my name . . ." The name of Jesus is the key card to open the door of answered prayer.

You could pray in the names of Buddha, Allah, Krishna, the mother Mary and many others and no change would come. (For the better anyway.)

When you pray in the matchless name of Jesus the authority resonates through both realms and answers must come.

R.W. Schambach was a powerful evangelist and a mighty man of God. He witnessed hundreds of thousands of miracles across the world during the span of his ministry.

During one crusade he wasn't satisfied with the results he was seeing at the altar and the stadium was not being filled. It seemed there was a hindrance in the predominantly Muslim nation where he was ministering.

When you pray in the matchless name of Jesus authority resonates through both realms and answers must come. #PraiseLaughRepeat

---

One night, as he was praying for the sick, a woman approached him who was completely blind. God gave him a divine idea. Turning to his interpreter he said, "Tell the crowd I'm going to pray for this woman in the name of Muhammad."

His interpreter was taken back and didn't want to say that. Finally, he relented and interpreted Brother Schambach's words.

Brother Schambach laid hands on the blind woman and prayed for her in the name of Muhammad. Nothing happened. He proceeded to pray in the name of Buddha, Krishna, and any other false god he could think of. Nothing.

"Now tell the people I'm going to pray in the name that's above every name," he said. When he prayed in the name of Jesus her eyes were instantly opened.

The next night the stadium was filled with people who heard what Jesus could do and many were saved.

There's power in the name of Jesus. Utilize the power of His name to receive your answered prayer and fullness of joy!

PRAYER POINT: Heavenly Father, intervene on my behalf today in the mighty name of Jesus. Stretch forth Your hand and bless every aspect of my life by Your mighty power.

11

LOOK BACK TO LOOK AHEAD

......

"When the Lord brought back his ex-iles to Jerusalem, it was like a dream! We were filled with laughter, and we sang for joy."

—PSALM 126:1–2 NLT

Today's Bible reading: Psalm 126:1–6

You have to have a selective memory. I don't mean the kind that every husband has been accused of having from time to time.

I'm talking about the events of your life. So many people have been taught to forget everything that happened before today and begin fresh every morning.

I've heard people make statements like, "Let the past stay in the past." In one sense, I understand what they mean. They are encouraging you not to dwell on the mistakes that are behind you. I agree that you cannot allow yourself to be bogged down by past failures.

Even the Apostle Paul said that he was focused on

"forgetting the past and looking forward to what lies ahead." (Philippians 3:13).

So you can't let previous mistakes prevent you from moving forward into what God has called you to achieve for His kingdom.

What I'm encouraging you not to forget are the wonderful things God has done in your life. Your personal testimonies are functional tools given by God to bring you victory and joy.

The people of Israel said that it wasn't until after God brought them out of captivity and back to their own land that their mouths were filled with laughter and they sang for joy.

Your personal testimonies are functional tools given by God to bring you victory and joy.
#PraiseLaughRepeat

According to the Word of God there are two components that give you full power to overcome the world. The first is the blood of the Lamb, and the second is *your testimony.* (Revelation 12:11).

Don't wait until your next blessing arrives from God to begin praising and thanking Him. Engage the force of praise and thanksgiving by looking back over your life and pointing out all of the wonderful things that God has done for you.

As I look back over my life, I can see things that no human being on the earth could have accomplished for me. I recognize the supernatural power of God and I thank Him for His intervention in my life.

Dr. David Oyedepo said, "Maybe the reason your next blessing hasn't come from God is because you haven't thanked Him for the last one He sent you."

Don't wait for a more favorable time. Begin to locate your testimony and praise God for His goodness today! As you do, the power to overcome is activated in your life and your mouth will be filled with laughter and singing.

....

PRAYER POINT: Heavenly Father, I thank You and praise You for all of Your goodness in my life. Help me to stay focused on your goodness and be grateful for your blessings each day.

....

DAY TWELVE

THE JOY OF THE INSTRUCTION MANUAL

*"Jesus told him, 'sell all your posses-
sions . . . Then come, follow me.' When
the man heard this, he went away sad,
for he had many possessions."*

— MATTHEW 19:21–22 NLT

Today's Bible reading: Matthew 19:16–30

We live in a society where nobody likes being told what
to do. The enemy has been hard at work to sow the seed
of rebellion into the world. The problem with a seed of
rebellion is that it always reaps a harvest of chaos.

God's Word is an instruction manual given to guide
us into success in every area of life. It gives us vision and
the ability to comprehend godly standards.

The Bible says that when vision is removed from any
group of people they perish. (Proverbs 29:18). Logically,
you would think the opposite must also be true: where
there is vision people will flourish.

Although the absence of vision ensures destruction,

vision alone does not ensure success. In *Praise. Laugh. Repeat.* I shared the story of my past frustrations during the Christmas season.

More than once I've overestimated my ability to put toys together for my daughters. After ripping open the packaging, I find myself tossing the instructions to the side and diving into the assembly of the pieces in the box. It never works. By the time I'm done, I could have saved tons of frustration and the desire to pour out my wrath with extreme prejudice on the toy if I had started with the instructions.

Vision alone is not enough to succeed. You have to submit yourself with obedience to instruction.
#PraiseLaughRepeat

Even Lego knows that you can't just buy one of their products, dump the pieces on your table, and put it together just by looking at the picture on the box. They include a very detailed, step-by-step manual that walks you through the assembly of the Legos.

Vision alone is not enough to succeed. You have to submit yourself with obedience to instruction.

King David was so thankful for God's Word. He understood that it was a lamp to guide his feet and a light for his path. (Psalm 119:105).

King David was a man of great success and a man who God loved. Although he made mistakes, the desire of his heart was to follow God's instructions and carry them out at all costs.

That kind of dedication brings the joy that David was constantly singing about.

Don't find yourself in the position of the rich young ruler of Matthew 19. When an instruction comes to you from the Word of God or the Spirit of God, realize it's your opportunity for great joy and success.

True joy is gained by seeking out God's instructions and completing them at all costs.

PRAYER POINT: Heavenly Father, remove any rebellion that may have taken root in my life. Empower me to receive your instruction with joy and carry it out with power.

13

DAY THIRTEEN

CROWS AND CANARIES

....

*"Don't live like fools, but like those who
are wise. Singing psalms and hymns
and spiritual songs among yourselves,
and making music to the Lord in your
hearts."*

—EPHESIANS 5:15, 19 NLT

Today's Bible reading: Ephesians 5:1–33

I found something interesting during my time research-
ing the subject of joy. People who are happy sing. Fur-
thermore, people who sing are happy.

So is singing the result of happiness, the cause of
happiness, or both? Surprisingly, both of these statements are true. It's widely accepted that if someone
comes down the street whistling or singing, we assume
they're happy.

In fact, the Bible says, "Are any of you happy? You
should sing praises." (James 5:13). It's not hard to sing
when you're happy and everything in your life is lining
up properly. Anyone can rejoice about victory.

The real test of your spiritual strength is when you can sing through battles, trials and attacks. God instituted singing to express joy you already have and to transport you into a realm of joy you've yet to attain.

A study published in Australia in 2008 revealed that on average, choral singers rated their satisfaction with life higher than the public — even when the actual problems faced by those singers were more substantial than those faced by the general public. Singing brings joy.

God instituted singing to express joy you already have and to transport you into a realm of joy you've yet to attain. #PraiseLaughRepeat

Our scripture for today says that we're not to live like fools, but like those who are wise. It goes on to say we should sing psalms, hymns and spiritual songs unto God. The writer is telling us that people who obey the command to sing unto the Lord are wise and those who refuse to sing are unwise.

I've heard people say, "I don't really sing because I'm not that good of a singer." They're referring to the fact that they're not skilled in the area of music. Maybe they find themselves singing flat or sharp and it's not pleasant to hear.

We have to keep in mind, however, that we're not singing to please people, we're singing to please God.

I heard one preacher answer a believer who was insecure in their singing abilities by saying, "God didn't just create canaries, He also created crows."

If all you can do is crow unto the Lord, that's what you should do.

The point of the *Praise. Laugh. Repeat.* message is that happiness is not a feeling, it's a choice. In the Psalms we find a command to "Serve the Lord with gladness. Come before Him, singing with joy." (Psalm 100:2).

You can't command yourself to have feelings, but you can determine your reactions. Employ the supernatural tool of singing today and engage the power of God in your life.

PRAYER POINT: Heavenly Father, I come to you today with singing and praise. Fill my mouth with a new song of praise and let it encourage someone today.

14

DAY FOURTEEN

STOP LIVING IN THE BALL PIT

*"For the Lord is the Spirit, and wher-
ever the Spirit of the Lord is, there is
freedom."*

— 2 CORINTHIANS 3:17 NLT

Today's Bible reading: 2 Corinthians 3:7–18

When I was growing up I loved going out to eat at fast
food restaurants. (Still do. Don't judge.) The thing that
made it even more exciting was getting there and find-
ing out that they had a play place inside the restaurant.

Every little kid secretly wishes they had a play place
right inside their room. Now that I'm a father, my own
daughters get excited about the play place.

As an adult, I didn't pay much attention to the play
place before I had children. I recently realized that these
aren't the play places of my youth. Something is missing.

The ball pit.

Many of you remember the ball pit. Sometimes positioned at the end of a long slide, the ball pit was supposed to be the grand finish to your ride.

It was a pool of colorful plastic balls. The ads showed children happily frolicking, splashing around and having a blast. It was an integral part of the play place.

I began to wonder why it was now absent. After doing some research I found that what seemed like an innocent tub of plastic balls was actually a cesspool of filth.

Inside the pit, workers would constantly find feces, old food, diapers, vomit, and the list goes on. One former worker released a report detailing the shameful cleaning methods used for the ball pit.

What seemed like a happy, fun place for your kids to play was actually a disgusting, and sometimes dangerous place to be.

The lives of many people are just like that. You could look into their home and everything seems fine on the surface level. Underneath that thin veneer, however, the enemy is wreaking havoc on their family.

Stop living in the ball pit.

The Bible gives us a clear solution in today's scripture. Wherever the Spirit of the Lord is there is freedom. If there is no freedom, it's because the Spirit of the Lord has not been allowed to function.

The Holy Spirit will not force you to let Him move in your life. You not only have to be open to Him moving, you must diligently seek Him in your daily life.

 If there is no freedom, it's because the Spirit of the Lord has not been allowed to function.
#PraiseLaughRepeat

You've got to create an atmosphere in your life that is conducive to the Spirit of God. Many of us waste valuable moments that could be spent seeking the presence of God. Why listen to a radio station on the way to work when you could be listening to the Word being taught. Why talk on the phone in the car when you could be talking to God?

When you make a conscious decision to diligently seek after God, He will surely reward you. (Hebrews 11:6).

PRAYER POINT: Heavenly Father, I'm seeking You today. Show Yourself mighty in my life and family. Fill my home with Your presence and bring everlasting freedom.

15

DAY FIFTEEN

EMPOWERED FOR EXPLOITS

....

". . . And many who had been para-
lyzed or lame were healed. So there
was great joy in that city."
— ACTS 8:7–8 NLT

Today's Bible reading: Acts 8:1–25

When I was seventeen years old I was asked to come
and speak at a youth camp in Missouri. Although I
knew I was called to preach, I had almost no experience
ministering.

I can remember being extremely nervous to preach
in front of hundreds of young people who were basically the same age as I was.

I was up very early studying on the morning I was
scheduled to speak. I wanted to make sure I had it all
together before I stood in front of that big crowd.

I remember preparing a message about getting bold
and taking your school for Jesus.

There was a young man at the camp who had been injured playing football the previous day. The camp leaders had taken him to the hospital and the doctor put his broken leg in a cast and gave him crutches.

As I was preaching my message that morning, that young man stood up and began walking toward the altar. He didn't even wait for the end of the service. He wanted to be prayed for immediately.

Faith brings miracles. Miracles bring joy. Joy brings strength.
#PraiseLaughRepeat

It was go time. I stopped preaching and told him to lift his hands. He stood there with crutches under his arms, hands raised and eyes closed.

I laid hands on him and commanded all pain to leave his leg. I asked God to supernaturally mend his broken bone by Holy Ghost power.

As soon as I prayed that prayer something changed in that young man's countenance. He threw his crutches down and began stomping on the ground with the foot that was in the cast.

The pain left his leg and God instantly healed him. All of the students began to rejoice and shout in their seats. I was probably the happiest person at the camp that day as I began my miracle ministry for the Lord.

The Bible tells us that the working of miracles brings great joy. As you read today's passage of Scripture, realize that when Philip was preaching and working miracles in Samaria he wasn't some mighty prophet of God. The Bible tells us that he was merely a believer who had been on the run from persecution.

Every believer is empowered to work the miracles of God. Step out in faith and pray for that sick coworker. Lay hands on your children and your spouse. Watch as God uses you to bring His miracle power to those in need. As these miracles take place, great joy will flood your heart.

....

PRAYER POINT: Heavenly Father, empower me today to work miracles. Use my life to heal the broken and bring deliverance to every captive.

....

16

DAY SIXTEEN

THE WATCHDOG OF YOUR HEART

·····································

"Don't worry about anything; instead, pray about everything. Then you will experience God's peace, which exceeds anything we can understand."

—PHILIPPIANS 4:6–7 NLT

Today's Bible reading: Philippians 4:1–23

When someone is giving you instructions it's important to pay attention. If they use the phrase, "whatever you do, don't. . ." that's when your ears should really perk up. They're about to tell you something that could be the life or death of your success.

The Bible is a book of instruction and wisdom. The book of Proverbs is like 31 chapters of concentrated wisdom. When you hear the writer of Proverbs say, "Above all else," you're about to get the pinnacle of wisdom.

That's just what he does in Proverbs 4:23 when he writes, "Guard your heart above all else, for it determines the course of your life."

Guard your heart.

If you're going to guard your heart, you need to know what will destroy it. Apparently, two of the biggest enemies of your heart are anxiety and fear.

The Apostle Paul tells the church that peace is the watchdog that stands at the door of your heart and guards it against the siege of anxiety and fear.

Peace guards you.

Not just any peace, supernatural peace. Paul describes it as, "peace which exceeds anything we can understand." What does that mean?

It means that ordinary peace comes when you know everything is okay. Nothing is out of place and things are running smoothly.

This is different. This is the kind of peace Jesus had when He was sleeping on a ship in the midst of a massive storm. The storm was so violent that the disciples, who were experienced men of the sea, were sure the boat was going down and they would all die.

In the midst of that extreme situation, Jesus didn't even wake up from peaceful sleep. This was not a yacht or a cruise ship. There were no plush cabins below deck. This was a fishing boat. Jesus was in the back, asleep on a pillow while rain and waves beat against his face. The wind was howling and the storm was raging.

He kept sleeping.

How do you get to a place in life where no storm can even shake you up?

Pray about everything.

When you obey the Word of God and spend time in prayer it releases a power into your life to walk in the peace of Heaven.

 Pray when everything is going smoothly and you can fly above every crisis situation.
#PraiseLaughRepeat

Don't wait for a crisis situation to engage the power of prayer. Instead, pray when everything is going smoothly and you can fly above every crisis situation.

Someone asked a minister if he ever had any problems. "Maybe they came and went," he replied, "but I never noticed." That's what prayer does for your life. It keeps you at a higher level than your enemy can fly.

PRAYER POINT: Heavenly Father, I thank You that Your peace surrounds me today and no enemy can infiltrate my heart and rob me of joy.

17

DAY SEVENTEEN

THE JOY OF GENEROSITY

....

"It is more blessed (makes one happier and more to be envied) to give than to receive."

— ACTS 20:35 AMP

Today's Bible reading: 2 Corinthians 9:1–15

Receiving a gift is wonderful, but there's nothing like the moment when you present a gift to someone that you know they'll really love.

A perfect example is watching your children opening their gifts on Christmas morning. Seeing them light up as they get just what they asked for is a gift in itself.

Nothing you can receive grants the same joy gained by generous giving. Giving is a higher way of living. Think about it logically. Everyone on the earth can receive something from someone. It doesn't take any special empowerment to receive.

However, not everyone is empowered to give at the

same level. Giving is a higher level than receiving.

It should come as no surprise to us that there is a supernatural joy attached to the act of giving. Jesus' words quoted by the Apostles are very interesting. People who give are more to be envied than people who receive.

That means we as believers should continually aspire to greater levels of giving.

When believers refuse to engage in generous giving, they are rejecting their heavenly DNA. The Bible says that God was moved by such passion for the world that He gave. (John 3:16). We are created in His image. When we submit to His image, we will give.

David was so moved by his love for God that he gave the largest offering in history. When others saw how much he gave, they began to give treasures also. The result? Great joy filled them all. (1 Chronicles 29:9).

When believers refuse to engage in generous giving, they are rejecting their heavenly DNA.
#PraiseLaughRepeat

When reading the story of the rich young ruler who came to follow Jesus, I find it interesting that Jesus tested his obedience in giving. Knowing that the man was controlled by his money, Jesus instructed him to sell his possessions and give them to the poor.

The story finishes with the rich man leaving with sorrow in his heart. (Matthew 19:21–22). The Lord spoke to me once and said, "When you refuse to obey an instruction to give, you don't just miss the harvest, you open the door and dismiss joy from your life."

Obeying the voice of God when He instructs you to give is a source of supernatural joy. Just as you set goals in other areas of your life, you should set giving goals as well. Purpose in your heart to give more each year.

As you do, expect your harvest to come and your joy to be full.

PRAYER POINT: Heavenly Father, give me faith to obey my divine instructions from Heaven. As I do, release overwhelming joy into my life

18

DAY EIGHTEEN

HEAVEN'S WRECKING BALL

....

> *"Around midnight Paul and Silas were praying and singing hymns to God . . . suddenly there was a massive earthquake . . . all the doors immediately flew open."*
>
> — ACTS 16:25–26 NLT

Today's Bible reading: Acts 16:16–40

It takes months to build a quality building the right way. There are many steps in the process that are necessary to make sure the building will be secure and safe to occupy. Plans have to be drawn, instructions followed, and measurements taken.

A demolition crew with a wrecking ball can destroy that same building in moments.

What took months to build can be destroyed in moments. Maybe the enemy has worked for months or years building his plans in your life. Maybe he has had control of your family for decades.

The good news is that Heaven's wrecking ball can

destroy what the devil has built in a matter of moments. Prayer, praise and thanksgiving are the three components that make up Heaven's wrecking ball.

As Paul and Silas began to pray and praise God, power from Heaven shook that building to it's very foundation and the doors came open without a key unlocking them.

 In a matter of moments, Heaven's wrecking ball can destroy what the devil has built in your life. #PraiseLaughRepeat

Prayer and praise combined can do what neither of them can accomplish alone.

When Paul and Silas began singing in the prison, I'm sure it seemed like an exercise in futility. They weren't just in a cell, they were in the inner dungeon. I'm sure those in charge felt confident that the Apostles would never escape.

I'm sure the prisoners inside their cells were annoyed having to listen to them sing.

The victory came as they combined the divine ingredients to the recipe: prayer and praise.

When they lifted up their voices in obedience and began to praise, something supernatural took place that night. The jail doors that their enemies trusted so much shook and opened wide.

Heaven's wrecking ball came down and destroyed the prison's capacity to retain it's prisoners.

Whatever you're dealing with in your life can be destroyed by the same power. Engage the weapons of prayer, praise and thanksgiving and watch as God destroys every plan of the enemy.

....

PRAYER POINT: Heavenly Father, stretch out Your mighty hand from Heaven and destroy everything the enemy has built up against me and my family today.

....

19

DAY NINETEEN

HE IS WHAT HE DOES

....

"Praise him for his mighty works;
Praise his unequaled greatness!"

—PSALM 150:2 NLT

Today's Bible reading: Psalm 150:1–6

I've been in plenty of church services and heard people
say things like, "I don't praise God for what He does, I
praise Him for who He is." The problem with this statement is that you cannot separate Who God is from what
He does.

In fact, even though His name is Jehovah, the Israelites in the Old Testament had to begin giving Him com-
pound names because of His mighty miracles.

When Abraham found out that God was his provid-
er he declared that God was *Jehovah-Jireh*, meaning the
Lord shall provide.

After Moses led the Israelites out of Egyptian captivity, God spoke to them and said He would allow none of the diseases that came on the Egyptians to touch them. On that day, God declared Himself to be *Jehovah-Rophe*, the God who heals you.

As you look down through the ages, you begin to realize He is what He does. God's names are shaped around the many aspects of His personality.

When anxiety, fear, or depression try to attack your life, you can give praise to *Jehovah-Shalom* Who is the God of your peace.

Whatever the enemy tries to throw at your life, you have a God Whose very nature combats every form of evil. Every wicked force has to respond to the power of His name.

As we see in today's verse, the book of Psalms instructs us to praise Him for His mighty works.

....

You have a God Whose very nature combats every form of evil.
#PraiseLaughRepeat

....

Just by the simple act of being obedient to this verse, you activate the miracle-working power of God in your life. God inhabits the praises of His people. (Psalm 22:3). When you praise Him, you are building a sanctuary for Him to live and operate in.

It's very dangerous to neglect your duty of praising God. A Christian who is praiseless is also powerless.

Give God something to work with today. Examine your life and discover where the enemy is trying to build a stronghold. Engage in praise to God for the aspect of His personality that will quickly deal with the situation.

We cannot praise Him for Who He is without praising Him for what He does. They are one and the same. Access His goodness today.

....

PRAYER POINT: Heavenly Father, show Yourself mighty in my life today. Make the wonders of Your personality real in my life as I praise You.

....

20

DO YOU KNOW WHO YOU'RE TALKING TO?

"They said to each other, 'Didn't our hearts burn within us as he talked with us on the road and explained the Scriptures to us?'"

— LUKE 24:32 NLT

Today's Bible reading: Luke 24:13–53

Have you ever sat and talked with someone for any period of time and realized that you're just not interested in anything they have to say? Not because you don't like people, but sometimes two individuals have nothing in common.

In fact, as they continue talking you feel yourself mentally leaving the conversation. You find yourself bored and looking for an excuse to leave no matter what subject they choose to talk about.

Nothing stirs within you.

There are other times when you feel the exact opposite. You may connect with someone you've never met and they feel like your long-lost best friend. As you sit and talk, everything they say excites you. When you look at your watch (or phone) you're amazed to see how much time has passed.

Why? There was an undeniable connection.

There is a certain connection that you cannot reproduce on the earth. When you connect to Jesus supernaturally, something is set on fire within your spirit.

This is a perk that some Christians never take advantage of throughout their life in Christ.

> People who have lost their fire for
> God have revealed that they refuse
> to spend time talking to Jesus.
> #PraiseLaughRepeat

The day of His resurrection, the disciples were joined by Jesus as they walked toward the city of Emmaus. They talked with Him all day long not realizing who He was. It was not until that evening as they ate together and He blessed their bread and then vanished that they realized Who they had been entertaining.

They made a very interesting statement as they noted the experience that should have tipped them off regarding His identity

"Didn't our hearts burn within us as He talked with us

on the road and explained the Scriptures to us?"

People who have lost their fire for God have revealed that they refuse to spend time talking to Jesus. As we've explored in previous entries, the overwhelming joy of the Lord can only be found in His presence.

When you spend time talking and connecting with the Spirit of God throughout your day, He will personally explain things to you about His Word that no one else can. He has answers regarding your life that can come no other way.

When you set an appointment with the Holy Spirit, He will never be late.

PRAYER POINT: Heavenly Father, reveal the secrets of Your Spirit to me and deposit Your fire in my heart today.

21

DAY TWENTY-ONE

SIN = SAD

....

*"Oh, the joys of those who do not fol-
low the advice of the wicked . . . But
they delight in the law of the Lord,
meditating on it day and night."*

—PSALM 1:1–2 NLT

Today's Bible reading: Romans 6:1–23

"I'm going to hell. In fact, I can't wait to get there. All of
my friends will be there and we're going to have a huge
party forever."

This is the thought process of some people today
and it's scary . . . and heartbreaking. The devil has de-
ceived the minds of many in our generation so that they
have no awareness of eternity.

In reality, sin is a job that will deliver a paycheck to
you. It's important to understand that the paycheck for
sin is not unhappiness. It's not missed opportunities.

The paycheck for sin is eternal death. (Romans 6:23)

The devil's mission statement has three clearly-marked goals. He wants to steal from you, kill you, and destroy your life.

Jesus, on the other hand, came to give you eternal, abundant life. (John 10:10).

Sin is a disease that kills everything it touches. It will destroy your job, relationships, finances, peace, joy and any other area it comes in contact with.

Sin is a disease that kills everything it touches. #PraiseLaughRepeat

The Bible makes a point to describe all of the joys of those who strive toward holiness. Psalm 1:3 says that the righteous will:

- Have a firm foundation.
- Continually produce fruit in every season.
- Never grow weak or brittle.
- Prosper in everything they do.

When you decide to go to war with sin, things have to change in your life. The areas that were dying will come back alive by the power of the Holy Spirit.

God spoke to the Prophet Isaiah and gave him a very simple stipulation: "If you are willing and obedient you shall eat the good of the land." (Isaiah 1:19 ESV).

The good of the land.

That's an important phrase. Obedience is not the only key to eating well. Willingness of heart is the other side of the coin. God doesn't want you to serve Him grudgingly. He wants you to serve Him with gladness. (Psalm 100:2).

The good of the land means that you will enjoy a hot, juicy steak while all the rebels are eating cold, over-cooked Ramen noodles.

Search your heart today. If anything could be found that's offensive to God, ask Him to remove it from your life. Your best days are just ahead.

....

PRAYER POINT: Heavenly Father, if there is anything offensive to You in my life, burn it away today. Create a clean, willing heart in me so that I can serve You with gladness.

....

22

DAY TWENTY-TWO

GOD WILL MAKE YOU LAUGH

....

"And Sarah declared, "God has brought me laughter. All who hear about this will laugh with me."

—GENESIS 21:6 NLT

Today's Bible reading: Genesis 18:1–15, 21:1–6

Have you ever been sick of seeing the same thing over and over and over? I was. Don't get me wrong, I was thankful for what God had been doing in my life and ministry, but I was ready for another level.

I'd read about great men of God who shut themselves away until God appeared to them and opened the door to the supernatural realm. I wanted God to do that for me.

I prayed a simple prayer. "God, I ask You to perform mighty miracles in our meetings and show people the reality of Your power."

Jesus didn't come in my room that day. God didn't

even take me on an journey through His Word to unlock the spiritual keys of power. He simply gave me one sentence, but that sentence changed my life.

"You've gone as far as you can go at your current level of prayer." It hit hard, but I didn't get offended. I remembered Jesus' response to His disciples when they failed to cast out an evil spirit.

"This kind can come out by nothing but prayer and fasting," He said. (Mark 9:29 NKJV). So that's what I began to do. The results have been wonderful.

One of the experiences that will forever be etched in my mind took place during a revival in Sussex, New Brunswick, Canada.

God's ability to make you laugh is directly connected to how often you talk to Him. #PraiseLaughRepeat

When I had finished preaching that night, I gave an altar call. A woman, who had never been to church before, came forward and gave her heart to the Lord. When she heard that we would be praying for miracles to take place, she ran to the children's class and grabbed her son and brought him to the altar.

Little, six-year-old Timothy had been blind in one eye for five years. When his mother brought him forward she said that she believed if I would pray for him God would open his eye.

I laid my hand on that precious, little boy and began to pray. I commanded that eye to open and see perfectly. When I took my hand off of him, he looked at me with a brand-new eye! When God performed that mighty miracle I began to weep and laugh at the same time.

What happened? God fulfilled Genesis 21:6 in my life. *God has brought me laughter. All who hear about this will laugh with me.*

Fasting and prayer will cause God to perform mighty miracles in your life. When He does, your mouth will be filled with laughter.

PRAYER POINT: Heavenly Father, show Your glory in my life as I seek Your face. Let others see Your miracles and cause them to laugh with me.

23

DAY TWENTY-THREE

THE MICHAEL JORDAN EFFECT

> *"So they went out quickly from the tomb with fear and great joy, and ran to bring His disciples word."*
>
> —MATTHEW 28:8 NKJV

Today's Bible reading: Matthew 28:1–10

A study published in the British Medical Journal, which followed almost 5,000 people over 20 years, found that happiness can spread through three degrees of separation within social networks, meaning that the happiness of your friend, your friend's friend, and even your friend's friend's friend can infect you with a good mood.

It's amazing to note the force of joy deposited inside the gospel as you read through the Word of God. Everywhere you turn, contagious, gospel joy spreads through those ancient cities and takes hold of people at a staggering rate. (Acts 8:8).

Paul gave us the diagnosis as to why the gospel has this contagious effect. He explains that the gospel is the power of God unto salvation. (Romans 1:16).

Let's experiment for a moment. I'm going to give you a few names and you see if you know what these people have accomplished. (No Wikipedia.)

Steve Kerr. Luc Longley. Will Perdue. Craig Hodges. None of these men ringing any bells? Do you know what they all have in common? They all played for the Chicago Bulls and won NBA championships alongside Michael Jordan.

The power of the gospel in your life will cause contagious joy to follow you wherever you go. People will feel it. #PraiseLaughRepeat

You don't know their names. In 1990-96 people barely knew their names. However, something happened to all of these men. They were sucked into the "Michael Jordan Effect."

People who have never watched one basketball game in their life know Michael Jordan. His leadership skills caused regular men to rise above their adversaries and conquer again and again. (Six times to be precise.)

His contagious abilities grabbed men at whatever

low level they were operating, and pulled them up to where he was living.

When you begin walking in the contagious power of gospel joy, you'll have the same effect on people that Michael Jordan did. It empowers you to lift others up to a level of victory required to overcome.

The power of the gospel in your life will cause contagious joy to follow you wherever you go. People will feel it. The women who were first given the gospel message ran from the tomb full of reverent awe and overwhelming joy. Allow the good news about Jesus to become your passion and drive your life.

PRAYER POINT: Heavenly Father, don't allow me to take for granted the wonderful gift of redemption that was purchased for me through the work of Christ. Empower me to spread it everywhere I go.

24

DAY TWENTY-FOUR

IGNORE THE WHINER

....

*"At that very time [Jesus] rejoiced
greatly in the Holy Spirit . . ."*
— LUKE 10:21 NASB

Today's Bible reading: Luke 10:17–28

You know the Whiner. That's the one who doesn't want
to get out of bed. The one who doesn't want to do anything with anyone because they're just "too tired." The
Whiner does what's easiest and feels the best. They don't
go to church because it's been a long week at work.

The list goes on and on.

You know the Whiner because it's you. It's all of us.
Our flesh to be more specific. In fact, our natural bodies are one of the biggest enemies of receiving spiritual
blessings. The Whiner doesn't rejoice unless it's convenient for him.

Dangerous.

Jesus rejoiced in the Holy Spirit. That should be an eye opener for us. The Apostle Paul knew the danger of letting his body dictate his life choices. He made a point to subject his body to the authority of God. (1 Corinthians 9:27).

Paul believed in this concept so thoroughly that he commanded the Philippians to ignore the Whiner: "Rejoice in the Lord always; again I will say, rejoice." (Philippians 4:4).

Isn't it interesting that he didn't begin by asking them which of them had recently won personal victories in their lives? He didn't ask who had just accomplished life goals. He said, "Rejoice!"

Never allow the outer you to control the decisions of the inner you. #PraiseLaughRepeat

It seems impossible that you could react to life's situations in a predetermined way. After all, you can't control your emotions right?

What Jesus did is the clue to solve this puzzle. He rejoiced in the Holy Spirit, not in his natural flesh or senses.

Christians are commanded to be filled with the Holy Spirit. (Ephesians 5:18). He is the source of joy. As we go a step further we see that the Bible instructs Spirit-filled Christians to sing praises and be consistently thankful for everything. (Ephesians 5:19–20).

This supernatural transaction bypasses the prison of fleshly feelings and allows you to enter the realm of heavenly reward.

Try it today. Rejoice in the Holy Spirit. You may have to start in a place that's naturally uncomfortable, but you will finish in joy. You'll end in strength because God inhabits the praises of His people.

....

PRAYER POINT: Heavenly Father, I dedicate myself to a life of constant praise and thanksgiving. The natural feelings of my body will no longer govern my reaction to Your goodness. I'll praise You today.

....

25

FOCUSED INTENSITY
....

"But seek first the kingdom of God and His righteousness, and all these things will be added to you."

—MATTHEW 6:33 ESV

Today's Bible reading: Matthew 6:1–34

Living in the blessings of God is never accidental. You can't trick God into blessing you. The Bible is clear that He only rewards those who diligently seek after Him. (Hebrews 11:6).

It's not a complex process. He doesn't pick and choose His favorites and bless them over His other children. The key to receiving God's blessing is to simply seek the kingdom diligently and with intensity.

A desire to please God is not what many Christians are lacking, rather, the intense focus to continue on that course.

Many times people seek God for a period of time

and see Him move in their life. When things are going well, they slack off in the seeking department. It's sad that it sometimes takes a desperate situation for people to begin seeking again.

You must intensely seek God when things are great just as much as when the enemy tries to launch an attack against you.

In his book *EntreLeadership,* Dave Ramsey shares what he calls the "Momentum Theorem." It's a simple equation that helps him explain the method to their constant success.

The formula is: *Focused Intensity over Time multiplied by God equals unstoppable Momentum.*

Intensely seek God when things are great just as much as when the enemy tries to launch an attack against you. #PraiseLaughRepeat

Every aspect of that formula is found in Scripture. Faithfulness is the Bible's term for focused intensity. Faithfulness to God's principles over time will always produce explosive results. (Read Joshua 1:8).

Many times what seems like an overnight success is just someone exploding onto the scene who has been employing that formula for years.

Laziness not only causes financial poverty, it causes spiritual poverty. You end up missing out on the blessings of God for your life. This is not because God doesn't want to bless you, but because you fail to seek Him diligently.

When God speaks to you to do something, you cannot wait for the most convenient time. When God spoke to me to release this devotional, it was an extremely busy season in our ministry. I couldn't just wait until I was locked in a quiet office with no distractions.

I'm writing this chapter in the passenger seat of my truck as my wife weaves it through traffic in the Bronx like a Nigerian taxi driver. Not the best conditions, but focused intensity keeps you on task until you accomplish the assignment that God has given you.

Decide today that you will seek His kingdom with unparalleled passion.

....

PRAYER POINT: Heavenly Father, inspire my spirit to react to Your kingdom principles not only when conditions are favorable, but at all times and in every season.

....

26

DAY TWENTY-SIX

THE POWER OF HIS PRESENCE

....

> *"A single day in your courts is bet-*
> *ter than a thousand anywhere else!*
> *I would rather be a gatekeeper in the*
> *house of my God than live the good life*
> *in the homes of the wicked."*
>
> — PSALM 84:10 NLT

Today's Bible reading: Psalm 84:1–12

God can do for you in one moment what men can't do for you in a lifetime. All of our work and effort means nothing if God's power is not connected to it.

The Bible says that unless the Lord is the One building the house, everyone else's work is in vain. (Psalm 127:1). Having God's power connected to our lives is the difference between struggling and sailing.

A sailboat doesn't require the same amount of work as a rowboat. The power and momentum of the wind gives you the extra boost to coast through the ocean.

Many people are trying to accomplish their purpose on their own. Without the assistance of God, however, you are struggling unnecessarily.

Our job is to open our sails and allow God to carry us supernaturally through our predestined path.

What men cannot do in many months, Jesus can do in moments. #PraiseLaughRepeat

This principle is perfectly illustrated for us in John chapter 6. Jesus is preparing to feed 5,000 men with five loaves and two fish.

Jesus turns to Philip and asks, "Where can we buy bread to feed all these people?" He was testing Philip, for He already knew what He was going to do.

"*Even if we worked for months*, we wouldn't have enough money to feed them," Philip said. (John 6:5–7).

Can you see the power of Jesus' presence in this story? Philip knew what a huge task feeding 5,000 men would naturally be.

What men could not do in months, Jesus did in moments. That's the power of His presence.

He is able to expedite His plan in your life.

If you've ever done any shopping on Amazon.com you might be familiar with Amazon Prime. When you sign up for this feature you get free two-day shipping on every order you place that year.

This is a great benefit, especially considering some of the item's standard shipping times are between four and fourteen business days.

Expedited is always better. As we rapidly approach the return of Jesus it's vital that we accomplish our purpose as quickly as possible.

Why neglect the presence of God and struggle through your life? Use the mighty wind of Heaven to your advantage.

Many people don't realize this is a benefit that comes from praising God. It causes you to be continually enveloped in His wonderful presence.

....

PRAYER POINT: Heavenly Father, as I spend time in Your presence, blow Your wind from Heaven and carry me through my purpose with supernatural momentum.

....

DAY TWENTY-SEVEN

HATERADE

....

". . . Michal, the daughter of Saul, looked down from her window. When she saw King David skipping about and laughing with joy, she was filled with contempt for him."

—1 CHRONICLES 15:29 NLT

Today's Bible reading: 1 Chronicles 15:1–29

If you've never heard the term *haterade*, it's a slang that has been defined as, "a fictional beverage, parodying the popular sports drink 'gatorade', purportedly consumed by individuals who are jealous of others, supposedly fueling their ability to 'hate on' others."

This is obviously what Michal was drinking in her ivory tower as she looked down with contempt on her husband David.

She should have been rejoicing with David, however, Michal was too caught up in the pride of their titles to be thankful for what was happening that day.

Victory was coming back to Israel.

There's one very important lesson we can learn from this story. Not everyone is going to be happy about the overwhelming joy that has come into your life.

Some people may be angry that you're finally happy. That sounds crazy, but it's true.

Sometimes people don't like it when those around them increase because it highlights the contrast between their lives.

Don't be discouraged if everyone you come in contact with doesn't celebrate your newfound joy. You can't please everyone.

There's a certain blessing God only releases when you're hated.
#PraiseLaughRepeat

I can remember people getting mad at me as a teenager because I was happy and would sing all the time. I actually had one person say, "What are you so happy about? Why do you have to sing all the time?"

Well, excuse me. I'm so sorry that my overwhelming joy interrupted your chronic depression.

There's a story in the book of Genesis about two sisters whose names were Rachel and Leah. Jacob wanted to marry Rachel because of her beauty, but because the oldest daughters were to be married first in that culture, their father tricked Jacob and gave him Leah.

When Jacob finally married Rachel, the Bible says he loved her much more than Leah. The Scripture goes on to say that when God saw that Leah was hated, He blessed her by opening her womb. (Genesis 29:31).

The Bible teaches that there is a specific blessing that God bestows upon you when you are hated by others. (Matthew 5:11). Some feel like the disapproval of others means that they're doing something wrong. On the contrary, unless you're being persecuted in some way, you're not doing it right.

Jesus said we would be hated all over the world for His name's sake. Don't be discouraged if everyone around you isn't as enthusiastic as you are about what God has done in your life.

God will use your life to touch and change them also. Be confident that no one can take away the eternal gifts that God has placed in your spirit.

PRAYER POINT: Heavenly Father, You are all I need. As I focus on You, give me the boldness to overcome every form of persecution in Jesus name.

28

DAY TWENTY-EIGHT

IT FLOWS FROM THE TOP

> *"The kings of the earth prepare for bat-*
> *tle; the rulers plot together against the*
> *Lord and against his anointed one. But*
> *the one who rules in heaven laughs."*
>
> −PSALM 2:2,4 NLT

Today's Bible reading: Psalm 2:1–12

One of the premiere rules of leadership is that it flows from the top down. The characteristics defining the leader at the top will be weaved throughout the entire organization.

If you work for a tense, angry boss, everyone in the office will also be tense and angry. The leader sets the tone.

I've talked with ministers who were frustrated with the people in their church because they seemed cold and disinterested in winning people to Christ.

I began to share with them how everything flows from the top. A leader always creates a direct reflection of himself in his people. Therefore, if the presence of God brings us into overwhelming joy, then God must also be filled with joy.

Some may think, *I've been a Christian for many years and I'm not filled with overwhelming joy.* I would encourage you to reevaluate whether you're truly following the Leader.

If you've been a Christian for years and are void of joy, reevaluate if you're following the Leader. #PraiseLaughRepeat

The Bible says that while evil men plot on earth to overthrow the plans of God and His anointed one, God sits on His throne laughing.

He's not overcome with grief or anxiety. He laughs. He knows that no weapon formed against Him can prosper, and the same is true for you. (Isaiah 54:17).

There's no need to be anxious about what may be going on around you.

Just laugh.

In the Old Testament an entire army showed up to kill one prophet named Elisha. When he and his servant woke up that morning they saw two different things.

The servant saw the horses, chariots and soldiers

holding their weapons. He was afraid and couldn't see a way out of the trouble.

Elisha, on the other hand, was calm and collected. He saw something different. He prayed that God would open his servant's eyes.

When they were opened, the servant saw what Elisha saw. There was an army of angels with chariots of fire surrounding their enemies. He realized there was no need for fear or panic. God was laughing on His throne. It's all a matter of what you can see.

Follow the Leader and laugh when the enemy threatens you with his meaningless deceptions.

PRAYER POINT: Heavenly Father, make me more like You. Empower me to walk in Your power and see what no one else can see.

FAN THE FLAMES

....

"This is why I remind you to fan into flames the spiritual gift God gave you when I laid my hands on you."

—2 TIMOTHY 1:6 NLT

Today's Bible reading: 2 Timothy 1:1–18

I can remember stepping out onto the basketball court in my mid-20's. This was a church league and I had been part of a state championship team a few years earlier.

These guys wouldn't be able to hang with me. I hadn't really practiced or played since high school, but basketball is like riding a bike, right? You don't forget.

The game started and I was running up and down the court. I was getting winded faster than I remembered. The crossovers that used to end successfully with a layup were now bouncing off of my shoe and out of bounds.

I pulled up for a jump shot near the free throw line

and watched in horror as I shot an air ball.

Where had my skills gone? I found out the hard way that if you don't stay on top of your gifts they can disintegrate very quickly.

This is true spiritually as well as physically. The Apostle Paul wrote a letter to Timothy, who was a younger minister, and encouraged him to fan his gift back into flames.

Locate what's wasting your time and take those moments to pray in the Spirit and fan your gift into flames. #PraiseLaughRepeat

This means that if neglected, your gift can die down and become stagnant. This also shows us that God doesn't control how potent our gifts become. Our own dedication to God's kingdom will determine how high we rise.

One of the best ways to fan your gift into flames is by praying in the Holy Spirit. The Apostle Paul told the church in Greece that when you pray in the Holy Spirit you are strengthened and built up personally. (1 Corinthians 14:4).

I have always made the analogy that praying in the Holy Spirit for a believer is like stretching for a runner.

No runner in their right mind just walks out onto the track, puts their feet in the blocks and waits for the gun-shot. They show up early, stretch and warm up.

The same thing happens in the Spirit. As you pray in the Holy Spirit you build up your faith. (Jude 1:20).

Spirit prayer is a necessity for the overcoming believer. In fact, the Apostle Paul said that he prayed in the Spirit more than anyone else. (1 Corinthians 14:18). There is a supernatural power attached to praying in the Spirit that can come no other way.

Locate whatever may be wasting your time and take those moments to pray in the Spirit and fan into flames the gift of God that's in you.

....

PRAYER POINT: Heavenly Father, don't allow me to become stagnant and disinterested in my gifts and calling. Stir me to pray and seek Your face like never before.

....

DAY THIRTY

TRADITION: THE JOY ASSASSIN

···

> *"But many of the older priests, Levites,
> and other leaders who had seen the first
> Temple wept aloud when they saw the
> new Temple's foundation. The others,
> however, were shouting for joy."*
>
> — EZRA 3:12 NLT

Today's Bible reading: Ezra 3:1–13

When God moves on and begins to do something new within a new season, you've got to move with Him. Those who stay behind become steeped in religious tradition.

When God speaks to you to make a change in your life or ministry, you've got to transition as quickly as possible. He said, "I am about to do something new. See, I have already begun! Do you not see it?" (Isaiah 43:19).

Although God's principles never change, His methods may differ depending on your situation. I like to remind people that Clorox bleach has had the same ingredients and product for 100 years, but they've changed the packaging many times to market to each new generation.

In today's Bible reading we see the picture of two types of people in the same tribe. First, the old generation who had seen the original temple of God in all it's glory. That was the high point of their life. Now that a new temple was being built they just grumbled and complained that it wasn't like the old temple.

The younger generation, who had never seen the old temple, were very excited about what God was doing in the present. They rejoiced as they built the new temple.

When you hold on to the past and don't move forward with God's new instruction, joy turns to sorrow. #PraiseLaughRepeat

The older generation should have been rejoicing as well. The important thing was not the temple building itself, but that God would dwell in their camp wherever they were.

The same thing happens today. I've seen people get mad at their church because they didn't like the song choices, there's too many lights on the platform, it's too loud, there's not enough hymns, and many other things.

The packaging may change, but we should all be thankful for the mighty presence of the Holy Spirit. As long as He is there, nothing else matters.

When you hold on to the past and don't move forward with God's new instruction, joy turns to sorrow.

If you're going to remain in overwhelming joy, you'll need to be continually led by the Holy Spirit. Something you heard from God ten years ago isn't going to cut it. It's a new day, and you need fresh manna from Heaven.

....

PRAYER POINT: Heavenly Father, make me sensitive to Your voice so that I can hear You as You lead me forward. Give me great faith to walk the steps You've laid out for my life.

....

DAY THIRTY-ONE

YOUR WEAPON FOR WARFARE

....

*"The Spirit of God, who raised Jesus
from the dead, lives in you. And just as
God raised Christ Jesus from the dead,
he will give life to your mortal bodies
by this same Spirit . . ."*

—ROMANS 8:11 NLT

Today's Bible reading: Romans 8:1–17

If you read Romans 8:11 in the old King James Version, it
says that the Holy Spirit will *quicken* your mortal body.

When I researched the Greek word translated
"quicken," I found that it could literally be translated
"to startle or make alive."

Have you ever been startled in the middle of the
night? Maybe you forgot you moved a piece of furniture
or your child left a toy on the floor. When you stub your
toe you go from being tired to startled and made alive.

One night, I woke up and got out of bed to use the
restroom. I was extremely tired and my eyes were barely open as I navigated the hotel room I was staying in by

the light of my iPhone.

I was so sleepy that my body felt twice it's weight. I dragged myself toward the bathroom door.

All of a sudden when I passed the closet I saw a full grown man standing in my hotel room with a flashlight in his hand.

Adrenaline shot through my body. I wasn't tired anymore. I was ready to fight for my life. I almost threw a punch with all the force I had in me.

 The power of the Holy Spirit creates a barrier that the worries of life can't penetrate to steal the Word. #PraiseLaughRepeat

Thankfully, I realized just in time that I was standing in front of a full-length mirror and was looking at a reflection of myself.

I just got quickened.

The Bible says that's the effect the Holy Spirit had on Jesus' dead body. The Spirit startled Him and shook His body back to life.

In the same way, we are made alive by the power of the Holy Spirit. His power is able to keep you from the cares of the world which rob you of His mighty Word. (Mark 4:18–19).

It's a mistake to view the Holy Spirit as God's side dish to the entree of salvation. Treating the baptism of the Holy Spirit as optional for the believer is essentially saying, "You're going to war. You can decide whether or not you'd like to take a weapon with you."

The Holy Spirit is our empowerment to overcome in every situation of life.

PRAYER POINT: Heavenly Father, fill me with the mighty power of the Holy Spirit and empower me to overcome every situation of life that the enemy would use to destroy me.

32

LOVE: THE ANXIETY BOUNCER

"There is no fear in love, but perfect love casts out fear. For fear has to do with punishment, and whoever fears has not been perfected in love."

−1 JOHN 4:18 ESV

Today's Bible reading: 1 John 4:1–21

Many people fail to realize how powerful the force of love really is. Love unlocks Heaven. Consider the rewards that are reserved for people who love God with their whole heart:

- God makes life line up for them. (Romans 8:28).
- He shows Himself mighty on their behalf. (2 Chronicles 16:9).
- Secret blessings are set aside for them. (1 Corinthians 2:9).
- God causes their enemies to be at peace with them. (Proverbs 16:7).

These are just a few of the many blessings that are outlined for people who love God with their whole heart.

The Apostle Paul said that if love isn't present in your life, every other good thing in your life amounts to nothing. (1 Corinthians 13:1–3).

When I read 1 John 4:18, the phrase, "perfect love casts out fear" always makes me imagine love as a bouncer tossing fear out of the building.

Love, like joy, is not a feeling or emotion, it's a fruit of the Spirit and therefore a choice.
#PraiseLaughRepeat

Love is obviously more powerful than the spirit of fear or it wouldn't be able to cast it out. In fact, when we realize that God is love, we understand why love is the greatest element throughout the Bible. (1 John 4:8).

Love, like joy, is not a feeling or emotion, it's a fruit of the Spirit and therefore a choice.

In the Old Testament there were over 600 laws that God's people had to remember to keep. Can you imagine trying to keep a checklist of over 600 things you had to remember to do, or not to do, every day?

I find it interesting that when Jesus came and fulfilled the Law of Moses, He replaced over 600 commands with just two.

Love God. Love people.

It's amazing how simple God made it for New Testament believers to please Him with their lives. Walk in love. The more you allow love to govern your life, the more fear has to leave it. Perfected love casts out every last bit of fear and anxiety. Decide to love like God loves.

PRAYER POINT: Heavenly Father, thank You for filling my heart with Your love. Let me constantly walk in love toward others and serve You with my whole heart.

33

AUTHOR. CHAMPION. JESUS.

> *"Let us strip off every weight that slows us down . . . And let us run with endurance the race God has set before us. We do this by keeping our eyes on Jesus, the champion who initiates and perfects our faith."*
>
> —HEBREWS 12:1-2 NLT

Today's Bible reading: Hebrews 12:1-13

The Apostle Paul received a powerful revelation from Heaven. Every blessing we have is given to us in and through Christ.

S.M. Lockridge, a Baptist pastor and world-renowned speaker, wrote about the aspects of these "In-Christ blessings" in his message, *That's My King.*

He said Jesus is the wellspring of wisdom, the doorway of deliverance, the pathway of peace, the roadway of righteousness, the highway of holiness, the gateway of glory, the master of the mighty, and the captain of the conquerors. The list goes on.

The verse we're focusing on today says that Jesus is

the author and the finisher of our faith. Those two facts should keep every believer in perfect peace.

First, Jesus is the author and creator of our faith. It's His design. He knows the ins and outs of every situation. Nothing troubles Him or throws Him into a panic.

Secondly, He is the finisher or perfecter of our faith. The same One who created it has the power to perfect it and finish it.

Because He is the Champion, we can keep our eyes on Him effectively stripping off every weight that would slow us down.

When you focus your life on Jesus, you're empowered to run a weight-less race.
#PraiseLaughRepeat

Paul said, "I press on toward the mark for the prize . . . " (Philippians 3:14).

No one is trained to run looking at the ground in front of them. Runners are trained to keep their eyes on a target. In a race, you keep your eyes on the person in front of you until you pass them, then you find a new mark.

The enemy wants to keep you looking at the things right in front of you. He wants you to focus on his smoke screen of deception. You've got to raise your eyes to Jesus Christ and run toward your goal. When you run with Christ as your focus, every weight must slide off of your shoulders.

Even the Apostle Peter stepped out of the boat onto the water and began walking toward Christ. As long as he kept his eyes on Jesus, he was weightless and did not sink. When his eyes began focusing on the waves, he began to sink.

Focus on Christ and run a weightless race.

PRAYER POINT: Heavenly Father, strengthen me to keep my eyes focused on You. Remove every weight from my life and keep me in perfect peace.

34

DAY THIRTY-FOUR

RECKLESS FAITH

....

*"The king appointed singers to walk
ahead of the army, singing to the Lord
and praising him for his holy splendor.
This is what they sang: 'Give thanks
to the Lord; his faithful love endures
forever!'"*

—2 CHRONICLES 20:21 NLT

Today's Bible reading: 2 Chronicles 20:1–30

Can you imagine being part of that conversation in 2
Chronicles 20? I would have loved to see the faces of the
people as they explained the plan.

"Okay here's what we want you to do. There's an
enemy army attacking us. We want you to get out in
front of the troops and as we march toward the enemy,
just begin to sing."

"That's funny, boss. Seriously though, what's the
plan? What weapons do I get?"

"Actually we're going to give you some musical in-
struments to play as you march and sing in front of the
army."

I'm sure more than a few people were freaking out.

The secret is, if you fight your own battles you can only fight as well as *you* can fight. When you engage the power and presence of God through praise, you can fight as well as *He* can fight because He fights your battles for you.

I would much rather have God fight my battles than fight them myself. He has never lost, and He never will. Even in what seemed like the devil's day of victory as Christ was crucified, God was winning.

To the point that the Bible says if the devil had known what he was doing, he would never have crucified Christ. (1 Corinthians 2:8).

When you engage the power and presence of God through praise, you can fight at God's level because He fights your battles for you.
#PraiseLaughRepeat

Reckless faith doesn't need to be in full control of every situation because it understands that God is in control.

Shadrach, Meshach and Abednego stood in front of the king and plainly declared that they would not bow their knees to him even if it meant their death.

Their faith was reckless. When the king tried to give them their punishment, Jesus showed up and fought their battle for them.

I'm encouraging you to jump out in reckless faith. No one should be satisfied living a spiritual life of carefully calculated risks.

Attack your purpose with such a solid trust in God that others watching would think you're irresponsible.

....

PRAYER POINT: Heavenly Father, I will trust in You no matter the natural circumstances. Fill me with boldness from Heaven to carry out my purpose on the earth.

....

35

DAY THIRTY-FIVE

A SHATTERING SHOUT

"Oh, clap your hands, all you peoples! Shout to God with the voice of triumph!"

—PSALM 47:1 NKJV

Today's Bible reading: Joshua 6:1–27

Have you ever shouted loudly in a public place and scared people around you? I have. Many times.

I felt the power of God once in Walmart and shouted in the frozen foods section. The only other person in the aisle was a white-haired, old lady. She promptly pushed her cart to another aisle.

There's something about a shout that carries power. As God's people, we're commanded to shout unto Him with a voice of triumph.

The mistake some Christians make is waiting until God performs a miracle in their life to shout.

Common sense says that if you're shouting before

the victory it's premature. Logically, you should save the celebrations for after the victory.

Did you ever consider that your shout secures the victory? I call it "The Shattering Shout." You can see it in action in Joshua chapter 6.

God instructed Joshua and his army to march around the walls of Jericho and then shout in triumph. As they did, the mighty walls of Jericho collapsed allowing them to run in and conquer the city.

 When you shout unto God, supernatural power is released to destroy the walls the enemy has set up to contain you.
#PraiseLaughRepeat

In the distinguished day and age in which we live, people may be hesitant to simply shout unto God. I assure you that I do it on a regular basis.

Joshua commanded the people, "Shout! For the Lord has given you the city!" When he said that, they were all still standing outside of a fortified barrier.

The key is to shout through any issue the devil has tried to raise up in your life.

The power of your shout will shatter the walls of his evil plans and they'll fall flat to the ground.

Shouting victoriously is simple faith in action. It tells the Lord that you believe He has already won the battle for you.

Shouts carry power. When Jesus shouted on the cross and released His spirit into Heaven, the earth shook and graves opened up. People were raised from the dead that day. (Matthew 27:50–53). His shout brought victory.

When He returns to rapture His church from the earth, He will descend from Heaven with a commanding shout. (1 Thessalonians 4:16).

Throughout the Bible, God shows forth His power through the Shattering Shout. Employ yours today and watch the walls crumble.

PRAYER POINT: Heavenly Father, don't ever let me become so dignified that I lose my shout. Work on my behalf and cause every evil wall to crumble in my life as I shout unto you.

DAY THIRTY-SIX

THE POWER OF HABIT

*"I will praise the Lord at all times. I
will constantly speak his praises."*
—PSALM 34:1 NLT

Today's Bible reading: Psalm 34:1–22

It's been said that you can make or break a habit in 21
days. Simply disciplining yourself to repeat the same
action over and over can cause it to become second nature to you.

God encouraged Joshua to create an obsessive habit
of studying and meditating on His Word. (Joshua 1:8).
God explained how that habit would cause Joshua to
prosper in everything he would do.

In 2012, author Charles Duhigg released a book en-
titled *The Power of Habit: Why We Do What We Do in Life
and Business.* During a Q&A session regarding the origin
of his book, Duhigg said:

"I first became interested in the science of habits eight years ago, as a newspaper reporter in Baghdad, when I heard about an army major conducting an experiment in a small town named Kufa.

The major had analyzed videotapes of riots and had found that violence was often preceded by a crowd of Iraqis gathering in a plaza and, over the course of hours, growing in size. Food vendors would show up, as well as spectators. Then, someone would throw a rock or bottle.

When you turn praise into a habit, victory becomes a lifestyle. #PraiseLaughRepeat

When the major met with Kufa's mayor, he made an odd request: Could they keep food vendors out of the plazas? 'Sure,' the mayor said. A few weeks later, a small crowd gathered near the Great Mosque of Kufa. It grew in size. Some people started chanting angry slogans. At dusk, the crowd started getting restless and hungry. People looked for the kebab sellers normally filling the plaza, but there were none to be found. The spectators left. The chanters became dispirited. By 8:00 p.m., everyone was gone.

I asked the major how he had figured out that removing food vendors would change peoples' behavior.

The U.S. military, he told me, is one of the biggest habit-formation experiments in history. 'Understanding habits is the most important thing I've learned in the army,' he said."

Habits change results.

When David wrote Psalm 34, he was making it clear that he would habitually praise God at all times and on every occasion.

When you turn praise into a habit, victory becomes a lifestyle. That's why the Bible has so much to say about praising God. The book of Psalms is basically a book dedicated to praising Him.

Throughout the entire Bible we have stories of the wonderful intervention of God when His people began praising Him.

Make praise a habit in your life today and God will show Himself strong on your behalf.

PRAYER POINT: Heavenly Father, I pray that my mind would continually be on You. Never let me forget the good things that You've done for me. Let Your praise always be on my lips.

DAY THIRTY-SEVEN

TAUNT YOUR GIANT

....

*"Today the Lord will conquer you, and
I will kill you and cut off your head.
And then I will give the dead bodies
of your men to the birds and wild ani-
mals, and the whole world will know
that there is a God in Israel!"*

—1 SAMUEL 17:46 NLT

Today's Bible reading: 1 Samuel 17:32–51

Giants deserve no respect. Go to YouTube, search *"Hulk
Hogan slams Andre the Giant,"* watch the video, and tell
me that something doesn't rejoice inside you.

In the Bible, giants represented the evil plan of the
devil for the world. They were the spawn of fallen angels and women.

Giants were not to be coddled and reasoned with,
giants were to be killed.

David was very irritated to see this giant standing
in the field and blaspheming the name of God. He was
baffled as to why no one had shut the giant's mouth.

His brothers, as well as the rest of the army, were

hiding out. They didn't want to get called out by Goliath. He was massive, scary and undefeated.

David simply had such a passion and love for God that he couldn't stand hearing that huge heathen running his mouth on the battlefield.

 Goliath wasn't a dangerous threat, he was a door to a throne. #PraiseLaughRepeat

David's faith caused him to taunt the giant. Goliath was David's giant because no one else would claim him. Goliath was a stepping stone to David's next level of victory. Goliath wasn't a dangerous threat, he was a door to a throne.

When the Israelites were given their Promised Land by God, it was inhabited by giants. They sent twelve spies on a recon mission.

When they returned, ten of them were discouraged because they saw how big the giants were. Joshua and Caleb, however, returned and said, "Let's go at once to take the land. We can certainly conquer it!"

Joshua and Caleb are the only two spies that most people can name. The other ten have been forgotten.

No one remembers the names of David's brothers who were hiding on the battlefield during David's fight with Goliath. Faith-filled action makes you memorable.

Today is the day to begin taunting your giant. Whatever the enemy has sent to destroy you will fall beneath you by the power of Almighty God.

When God reveals His promises to you, your first response should be, "Let me go at once to take the land. I can certainly conquer it!"

....

PRAYER POINT: Heavenly Father, let the same boldness that filled David, Joshua and Caleb fill me today. Anoint me to take the promises You have set aside for me.

....

38

DAY THIRTY-EIGHT

KICK THE DOUBT OUT

"The crowd laughed at [Jesus]. But he made them all leave, and he took the girl's father and mother and his three disciples into the room where the girl was lying."

—MARK 5:40 NLT

Today's Bible reading: Mark 5:1–43

Many times when people picture Jesus they imagine a very soft-spoken, non-offensive man floating around in glowing robes.

Jesus may have been meek and humble, but He carried power and authority.

When a man named Jairus traveled to see if Jesus would come heal his daughter, Jesus responded with compassion and went to Jairus' house.

When they arrived, his daughter had already died and people were mourning her.

Jesus asked, "Why all this commotion and weeping? The child isn't dead; she's only asleep."

The crowd began to laugh and make fun of Jesus. So you know what He did?

Jesus kicked them out.

Doubt is the most dangerous element in the world. It short circuits the power of God. When Jesus went back to His hometown, He couldn't even perform miracles because of all their doubt. (Mark 6:5).

Doubt is the enemy of a miraculous Christian life. Kick it out as soon as you see it. Don't let it stay.

Jesus finished by raising the little girl from the dead. Some people may have thought Jesus was insensitive that day, but unless He corrected the atmosphere, the parents would never have regained their daughter.

Doubt is the enemy of a miraculous Christian life. Kick it out as soon as you see it. #PraiseLaughRepeat

It's life or death what type of atmosphere you cultivate in your life. If doubt can steal your opportunity for God to miraculously intervene in your life, it has also stolen your opportunity for overwhelming joy.

In *Praise. Laugh. Repeat.* I showed you from the Word of God that when miracles take place, it causes joy to flow freely. (See Acts 8:5–8).

God gave us the remedy for the disease of doubt. It

is the power of His Word. Faith comes by hearing the Word of God preached. (Romans 10:17).

There's no excuse for having no faith in our generation. The internet is such an incredible resource. You can watch powerful men of God all over the world.

It's a privilege to live in a time where knowledge has greatly increased just as the Bible predicted. We should take advantage of all the opportunities presented to us before Jesus comes.

Take intentional steps to build your faith so that doubt cannot hold you hostage when miracles should be flowing in your house.

Build your faith. Grab your miracles. Walk in joy.

....

PRAYER POINT: Heavenly Father, supernaturally strengthen my faith as I read and listen to Your Word. Remove all doubt from my heart and perform miracles in my life.

....

39

DAY THIRTY-NINE

PEACE BOOSTS YOUR SIGNAL

....

*"For you will go out with joy and be
led forth with peace;"*

—ISAIAH 55:12 NASB

Today's Bible reading: Isaiah 55:1–13

Have you ever seen someone trying to break a piñata?
They're blindfolded, spun in circles until dizzy, and set
loose while everyone is yelling and screaming instructions.

It's funny to watch the person swinging wildly hop-
ing to hit the target. They know there's a stash of candy
inside if they can just break the piñata open.

Without the blindfold, dizziness, and confusion, the
job would be simplified. Peace and joy are the twin tools
that simplify your goals for you.

Joy is the fuel that strengthens you for the task at
hand. You are able to accomplish your tasks with force

and momentum. In a sense, it removes instability and let's you move forward in power.

Peace is the tool that removes the blindfold and quiets the crowd. Once that has happened, you can hear the voice of the Holy Spirit clearly as He directs you to your spiritual candy-filled, paper mache donkey.

Joy empowers you to go, peace allows you to be led. (Isaiah 55:12). It's hard to hear the Spirit of God when the anxieties and frustrations of life are yelling inside your mind.

Peace is needed to enter your divine rest. The wonderful thing about hearing the Spirit's instruction and obeying it, is that it ensures you're working on His project and not yours.

If you're void of peace from carrying a heavy load, you didn't get it from God. #PraiseLaughRepeat

Unless you team up with God, the Bible says your work is useless. (Psalm 127:1). It's prideful for us to attempt to do everything on our own.

God has a plan. When we submit to it and obey each instruction, He will give us supernatural rest. (Psalm 127:2).

God hasn't called us to suffer and struggle through

our calling and purpose. Jesus instructed us to come to Him if we were weary or weighed down and He would give us rest. He said that His yoke is easy and His burden is light. (Matthew 11:30).

If you're void of peace from carrying a heavy load, you didn't get it from God. In fact, when you carry out God's plans in perfect obedience, you can see breakthroughs without sweat.

....

PRAYER POINT: Heavenly Father, as I access Your joy and peace, speak to me today. Let me be sensitive to Your voice so that I can carry out Your plans.

....

DAY FORTY

X MARKS THE SPOT

....

"And now I commend you to God and to the word of his grace, which is able to build you up and to give you the inheritance among all those who are sanctified."

— ACTS 20:32 ESV

Today's Bible reading: Acts 20:17–38

Today is the final day of this devotional, but it's the first of many days of overwhelming joy for you. This devotional is not the end of your experience, rather, a primer to set you on the right course.

Today's verse tells us that it is the Word of God that is able to build you up and give you your inheritance. It's very plain to see that many are not holding their inheritance because they're not being built up by God's Word.

You must understand that the revelation of God's Word comes in different levels of power. It's not all the same. In fact, the only way to attain higher levels of power is to access higher revelation of the Word.

Did you know that the Apostle Paul was frustrated with the Christians in Greece because they could only handle lower levels of God's Word? He wanted to give them more powerful revelation, but they couldn't handle it. (1 Corinthians 3:2).

The Word of God is spiritual nutrition. The more you ingest, the stronger you become.
#PraiseLaughRepeat

We understand that the Word of God is spiritual nutrition. The more you ingest, the stronger you become. There are six levels of spiritual nutrition found in the Word of God:

1. The Water of the Word. (Ephesians 5:26).
2. The Milk of the Word. (1 Corinthians 3:2).
3. The Bread of the Word. (John 6:48).
4. The Strong Meat of the Word. (Hebrews 5:13).
5. The Honey of the Word. (Proverbs 24:13-14).
6. The Wine of the Word. (Genesis 49:9,12).

Obviously, water and milk won't do for you what bread and meat will do. You are responsible to continue increasing in the strength of God's Word. The more Word content you digest spiritually, the more of your heavenly inheritance you'll be holding in your hands.

I'm encouraging you to become a voracious reader of the Bible. Study it. Think about it. Obey it. Live it.

As you do, you will increase in spiritual power and authority. Ultimately, joy comes from being in union with God's desires and commands for your life.

Stay on course. Nothing is going to hinder you in accomplishing your purpose.

PRAYER POINT: Heavenly Father, give me a spirit of wisdom and revelation as I study Your Word. Let me grow in spiritual maturity so that I can increase my spiritual nutrition level and secure my inheritance.

ABOUT THE AUTHOR

TED SHUTTLESWORTH JR. has been involved in full-time ministry since he was a child. He began traveling on the road with his father and mother at the age of two weeks old. Five years later in a small church in Northern Maine, Ted felt the call of God on his life.

Ted has been preaching the gospel for close to two decades. As a third-generation minister, the responsibility to reap this end-time harvest of souls has been ingrained in him since childhood. The focus of Miracle Word Ministries is to preach the Word of God, see the Salvation of the Lord, and bring the miraculous power of Jesus Christ to a hungry generation.

Ted is a graduate of Rhema Bible Training College and currently resides in Virginia Beach, Virginia, with his wife, Carolyn, and their daughters Madelyn and Brooklyn.

JOIN THE CONVERSATION ON SOCIAL MEDIA

@tshuttlesworth /MiracleWordMinistries

PRAYER OF SALVATION

Heavenly Father,

Thank you for sending your Son, Jesus, to die for me. I believe that You raised Him from the dead and that He is coming back soon.

I'm asking you to forgive me of my sin and make me brand new. Give me holy desires to pray and read your Word. Empower me by Your Holy Spirit to live for You for the rest of my life.

You are the Lord of my life. I thank you that the old life is gone and a new life has begun, in Jesus Name, Amen.

If you prayed this prayer, please contact us. We would like to send you a free gift, pray for you and help you take your next steps in Christ.

info@miracleword.com